ATHENEUM BOOKS FOR YOUNG READERS

An imprint of Simon & Schuster Children's Publishing Division

1230 Avenue of the Americas, New York, New York 10020

For information about special discounts for bulk purchases, please contact Simon & Schuster Special Sales at 1-866-506-1949 or business@simonandschuster.com.

The Simon & Schuster Speakers Bureau can bring authors to your live event. For more information or to book an event, contact the Simon & Schuster Speakers Bureau at 1-866-248-3049 or visit our website at www.simonspeakers.com.

Book design by Debra Sfetsios-Conover

The text for this book is set in Franklin Gothic Book.

The illustrations for this book are rendered digitally.

Manufactured in China

0411 SCP

First Edition

10 9 8 7 6 5 4 3 2 1

Library of Congress Cataloging-in-Publication Data

Campbell, Eileen, 1956–

Charlie and Kiwi / by Eileen Campbell and Judy Rand ; illustrated by Peter H. Reynolds ; with New York Hall of Science and FableVision. — 1st ed.

p. cm.

Summary: Charlie, who wants to explain to his classmates why the kiwi is so different from other birds, follows his stuffed friend Kiwi on a journey through time on which one of his ancestors helps him understand how the kiwi—and all birds—evolved.

ISBN 978-1-4424-2112-7

[1. Kiwis—Fiction. 2. Birds—Fiction. 3. Evolution—FIction. 4. Space and time—Fiction. 5. Great-grandfathers—Fiction. 6. Schools—Fiction.] I. Rand, Judy. II. Reynolds, Peter, 1961– ill. III. New York Hall of Science. IV. FableVision Studios. V. Title.

PZ7.C15097Ch 2011

[E]—dc22   2010042905

Acknowledgments

This story was developed as part of a traveling exhibition called *Charlie and Kiwi's Evolutionary Adventure*. The development team for this project included:

Project director and content research

Martin Weiss, PhD, New York Hall of Science, PI

Research children's concepts of evolution and natural selection

E. Margaret Evans, PhD, University of Michigan, Co-PI

Conceptual design, illustration, and exhibition development

Sean Duran, Miami Science Museum, Co-PI

Education support material development

Margie Marino, North Museum of Natural History and Science, Co-PI

Exhibition development and design

Jeff Kennedy, Jeff Kennedy Associates, Inc.

Narrative story and interactive exhibition development

Margie Prager, Jeff Kennedy Associates, Inc.

Writing and exhibit development

Judy H. Rand, Rand and Associates, and Eileen Campbell, Farallon Media

Audience evaluation of the narrative story

Martin Storksdieck, National Academy of Sciences, and Judy Koke, Ontario Art Gallery

Illustrations, animation, and production of the story

Peter H. Reynolds and FableVision, Inc.

This material is based in part upon work supported by the National Science Foundation under Grant Number ISE 0540152. Any opinions, findings, and conclusions or recommendations expressed in this material are those of the author(s) and do not necessarily reflect the views of the National Science Foundation.

Peter H. Reynolds and New York Hall of Science present

Written by Eileen Campbell
Illustrated by Peter H. Reynolds & FableVision

CHARLIE and KIWI

an Evolutionary
Adventure

Atheneum Books for Young Readers
New York · London · Toronto · Sydney

This is **Charlie**.

Charlie has to write a report
for school. **About a bird.**

He knew everyone else would write about robins
and eagles and blue jays. Charlie wanted something
different. Something a little surprising.

His kiwi, of course!
His parents had brought the stuffed
animal home from New Zealand.

"A very odd bird,"
Mom had said when he opened
the box. Charlie loved it.
And he still had the box,
with lots of facts on the back.

Kiwi was even easy
to draw. **Perfect!**

The next day Charlie started his report.

"The kiwi!" he began.

THE KIWI

"It's supposed to be about birds,
not fruit!" someone called out. Lena, of course.

But Charlie was prepared.
He pulled Kiwi from his
backpack with a flourish.
Everybody laughed.

"Izzat a *bird*? Where's
the wings?" Jack snickered.

"Of course it's a bird—
a really cool bird!"
Charlie said. "The kiwi
doesn't fly. It's different. It's
got whiskers and—"

"Whiskers?!" Maggie
shouted. "How can that be
a bird? Maybe it's a cat!"

"Settle down, class," said the
teacher. "Let Charlie tell us *why*
the kiwi is different."

Uh-oh, thought Charlie as he stared at his report.

It had all the facts:

✔ Kiwis don't fly.

✔ Kiwis have teeny tiny wings, furry feathers, and big feet.

✔ Kiwis come out at night.

✔ Kiwis have a great sense of smell.

But *why* was a kiwi so different from other birds? He didn't know.

He needed answers—fast!

Just then, the bell rang. "You can finish tomorrow, Charlie," the teacher said.

Charlie stayed up late that night, reworking his report.
"I have to show the kids you really *are* a bird," Charlie muttered to Kiwi.

A tiny motion caught his eye. Had Kiwi nodded?

"A really *cool* bird," Charlie said.
Kiwi *definitely* nodded.

Charlie squinted at Kiwi. "And why is a kiwi **so different**?" he asked.
"Why don't *you* tell me?"

Kiwi didn't move.

"Right, I'm asking a stuffed animal," Charlie said, yawning. "It's hopeless."

Suddenly, Kiwi jumped into motion.
She tap-tapped her long beak twice on the photo of
Charlie's Great-Great-Great-Great-Great-Grandpa, the
bird expert. Then she popped into her box.

Astonished, Charlie grabbed the box and . . .

"Keeee-weee! Keee-weee!" called Kiwi.

At that, they were zooming through space.
The years flashed by on a screen:

2011!

2000!

1990!

1980!

At **1860**, the box shuddered and shook and stopped with a **thump**.

Charlie and Kiwi had landed in a room full of books and pictures of birds—and a peculiar old fellow who seemed startled to see them.

"I was expecting dinner," he said, eyeing Charlie.
"You're not my dinner."

The old fellow looked a bit . . . familiar.

"Are you my Great-Great-Great-Great-Great-Grandpa Charles? **The bird expert?**" asked Charlie.

"Birds, yes," he replied.

"Your five-times-great-grandfather? Well, maybe. **My name *is* Charles.** And you *do* have my nose. And some kind of Time-Travel Contraption, apparently."

"And you have a kiwi!" he added
approvingly.
"Wonderful birds!"

Kiwi beamed.

"So you know about kiwis!" Charlie said. Things were looking up. "I need to **prove the kiwi's a *bird*.**"

"Well, **of course** a kiwi is a bird," said Grandpa Charles. "It's got feathers, a beak, and two legs."

Kiwi nodded.

"But kiwis don't fly!" Charlie said, the sound of his snickering classmates still fresh in his ears.

"Some birds **don't fly**," explained Grandpa Charles. "Kiwis, penguins, and ostriches."

Kiwi nodded again.

"But why not?" asked Charlie.

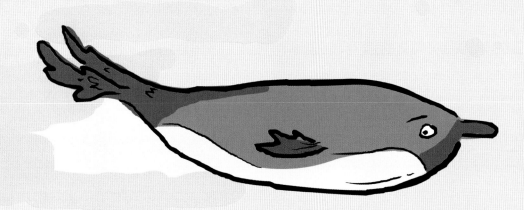

"We know that **birds changed** by looking at their ancestors, like this ancient fossil.

"But we don't have a kiwi fossil.
You'd have to go see for yourself. Go a long, **looong** way back in time. Back to the very first kiwis, on the island of New Zealand."

"Keeee-weeee! Keee-weee!"
Kiwi called them into the box.
Charlie followed.

"But it's time for my dinner!"
Grandpa Charles protested.

Too late. The three of them were
already zooming through space:

5 million!

10 million!

20 million!

At **30 million years ago**,

the box shuddered and shook
and stopped with a **thump**.

Charlie looked around.
"I don't see any kiwis," he said.

"No, but **watch out** for eagles!"
Grandpa Charles grabbed Charlie
as an enormous bird swooped out of
the sky. "On islands, hawks and eagles
are the big predators, instead of wolves
or lions."

"Kiwi can't fly!" Charlie said, alarmed.
"The eagle will get her!"

But Kiwi had run to a clump of tall grass. Hidden, she was safe. The eagle squawked off, chasing another bird.

"Pretty smart, Kiwi," said Charlie, relieved. "If it's dangerous in the air, maybe it's better not to fly. Maybe kiwis don't really **need** wings."

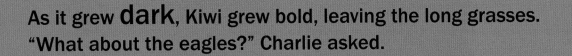

As it grew **dark**, Kiwi grew bold, leaving the long grasses. "What about the eagles?" Charlie asked.

"Eagles hunt during the day," Grandpa Charles explained. "At night, kiwis are **safe**."

Charlie watched Kiwi poking her beak around in the leaves. "Whiskers are good for feeling your way in the dark, like cats do," Charlie said.

"That's how she catches dinner!" said Grandpa Charles as Kiwi snapped up a fat bug. "Ah . . . **dinner**," he added wistfully.

Watching Kiwi catch bug after bug,
Charlie started to see *why* kiwis are so different.

Shy Kiwi had turned into
a superior night-striding,
no-flying, big-bug-hunting bird.

"She's *just right* for
life in New Zealand!"
said Charlie.

"I still don't know
how kiwis got this way."

"Hmm. Well, I have a theory,"
confided Grandpa Charles.

"**Long ago**, maybe kiwis were more like regular birds.
Maybe they had wings and flew.
But say one family was a little bit different.
Say some stayed on the ground a little more and smelled bugs
a little better. They'd be safer, and catch more dinner. . . .

"The Little-Bit-Different family would raise more chicks.

"Their chicks would be a little different, too. Each generation would fly less, stay up later, get better at sniffing out bugs. Each generation would be a little better for life in New Zealand.

"Eagles would keep catching the flying, awake-in-the-day, not-so-different birds. So there'd be fewer of them in each generation— and more of the Little-Bit-Different ones.

"Little changes in each generation add up to **big changes**. So over a long, **looong** time and many, **many** generations, the Little-Bit-Different ones give rise to a *very* different kind of bird: the kiwi!"

Kiwi did a little dance.

"That's pretty cool," said Charlie.

But was it cool enough? He looked at Kiwi—those big feet, those whiskers.
Jack was still going to say, "Izzat *really* a bird?"

"I *have* to find out what a bird really is," said Charlie.
"We need to go find the **very first bird**."

"The very first birds? That would be a long, long, **long, LOOONG** way
back in time," said Grandpa Charles.

Charlie was already in the Time-Travel Contraption. "Keeeeeee-weeeee! Keeee-weeee!" commanded Kiwi.

And **back** they went:

50 million!

75 million!

100 million!

At **150 million years ago**,

the box shuddered and shook and stopped with a **thump**.

"Oh dear," said Grandpa Charles, looking around. "I'm afraid we're a long, long, long, *looooong* way from dinner."

Charlie wasn't listening. He'd seen something amazing.
"A DINOSAUR!" he exclaimed. "At least, I think it's a dinosaur.

"It has **claws and teeth**, like a dinosaur. But . . . are those feathers?"

Grandpa Charles was puzzled too. "**Feathers?** That should mean it's a bird. It runs on two legs, like a bird. But . . . it's got teeth instead of a beak. If it is a bird, it's a really odd bird!"

"It's not a bird, it's a *dinosaur*!" Charlie said.
"Some ran on two legs—like *T. rex*.
But why would a dinosaur have feathers? They **don't fly**."

"Hmm," said Grandpa Charles.
"Feathers aren't just for flying.
Downy feathers keep birds warm.
But look—some of the dinosaurs
have feathers that are
a *little bit* different. . . ."

Charlie crept closer.
"Yeah, they're a little longer
and stiffer. And when *those*
dinosaurs jump to catch bugs,
they kind of . . . glide."

"And they catch dinner a little bit better,"
said Grandpa Charles appreciatively.
"They'll have more food to feed their babies."

"And more of the long-feathered babies
will survive to have long-feathered babies
of their own," Charlie concluded.

"I think you're getting it, my boy!" Grandpa Charles exclaimed. "A little change like that, in each generation, would—"

"Let's go see!" shouted Charlie. They looked at Kiwi.

"Kee-wee! Kee-wee! KEE-WEE!" she called. And off they went— forward in time this time.

Peering out the window, Charlie and Grandpa Charles watched the world change. There were more feathered dinosaurs in each generation. They had more feathers, longer feathers, stiffer feathers.

Little changes adding up to **big changes**.

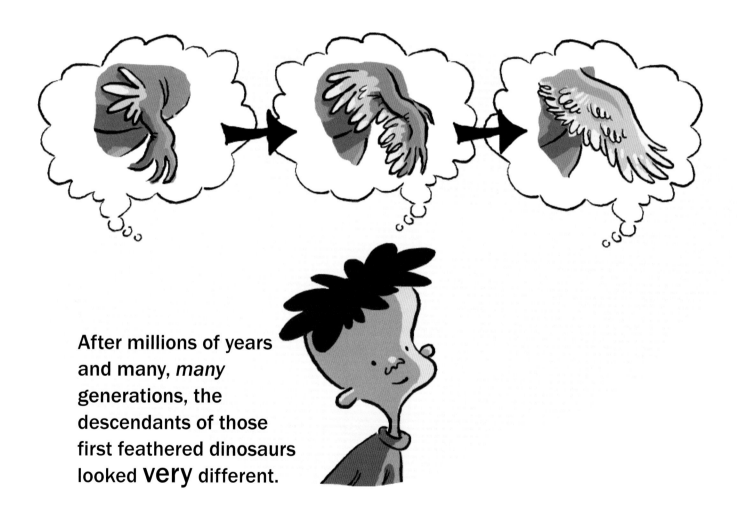

After millions of years and many, *many* generations, the descendants of those first feathered dinosaurs looked **very** different.

"**Stop here!**" said Charlie.
He leaped from the box.
"Whoa! Now they can fly!"

"Fascinating!" said
Grandpa Charles.
"This dinosaur looks
a lot like a bird."

"Maybe it **is** a bird," said Charlie. "It's one of the very **first** birds!"

"So the first birds were dinosaurs—with feathers!" they shouted together.

Kiwi did a little dance.

"And over time, the first birds evolved into thousands of kinds of birds!"
Now Grandpa Charles was dancing like Kiwi. "Robins, eagles, blue jays.
Pelicans. Peacocks . . . penguins and ostriches!"

"And KIWIS!" shouted Charlie. "Kiwi—you're a kind of *dinosaur*!
And you're a bird. Nothing's cooler than that! Wait till the kids hear this!"

And so they **zoomed home**, stopping once to drop Grandpa Charles in his study in 1860. "You'll need proof!" said Grandpa Charles. "Take my fossil!"

The next morning Charlie stood in front of his class, telling them about his adventure with the night-striding, no-flying, big-bug-hunting kiwi who was *just right* for life in New Zealand.

This time the class didn't laugh.

"So that's why kiwis are like kiwis," Charlie explained. "And why kiwis—"

"And penguins!" called out Lena.

"**And eagles!**"
Jack added.

"**And robins!**" said Maggie.

"**And every bird is different**, but all part of one big, **amazing family**. And if you could go way, *way* back in time, you'd see that *all* birds came from the same ancestor: **the *dinosaur*.**"

"Dinosaurs. Whoa," they all said. Everyone was looking at Charlie, impressed.

They didn't see Kiwi nod.
But Charlie did.

Meanwhile, back in 1860, Grandpa Charles had something new to think about.

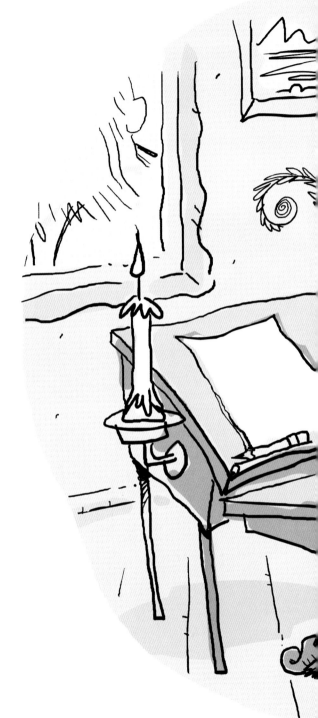

"So if birds came from dinosaurs . . .
I wonder if **dinosaurs taste like chicken**?

"Say, where's my dinner!?!"